P9-DGD-026

629.133 VIN

Vines, Mike.

Wind in the wires

Please check all items for damages
before leaving the Library.
Thereafter you will be held
responsible for all injuries
to items beyond reasonable wear.

Helen M. Plum Memorial Library

Lombard, Illinois

A daily fine will be charged for
overdue materials.

OCT   2000

The Fairey Swordfish, known
affectionately to everyone who flew in or
serviced it as the 'Stringbag', was
virtually obsolete when war broke out in
1939. This example, a Swordfish II, LS326,
is one of two flying examples in the UK
proudly operated by the Royal Navy
Historic Flight at RNAS Yeovilton. These
carrier-borne aircraft were slow, stable,
and very manoeuvrable, and therefore
ideal platforms for launching torpedoes
and bombs. They were involved in many
famous naval engagements during World
War II, in particular the night attack on the
Taranto dockyards when two Italian
battleships were sunk and another
severely damaged as well as a cruiser,
two destroyers, some seaplane hangars
and oil storage tanks. Another famous
engagement took place in the Atlantic
where the Royal Navy were hunting the
German battleship *Bismarck*. Swordfish,
from HMS *Ark Royal* and *Victorious*,
attacked the huge vessel and disabled its
steering gear with their air-launched
torpedoes – the *Bismarck* was then
finished off by the fleet.

WIND
IN THE
WIRES

Mike Vines

Helen Plum Library
Lombard, IL

MBI Publishing Company

629.133
VIN

DEDICATION

This book is dedicated to the memory of Cole Palen, Aviator and Showman.
1926 – 1993

This edition first published in 1995 by Motorbooks International, Publishers & Wholesalers, PO Box 2, 729 Prospect Avenue, Osceola, WI 54020, USA.

Reprinted 1999

© Mike Vines 1995

Previously published by Airlife Publishing Ltd, Shrewsbury, England, 1995

All rights reserved. With the exception of quoting brief passages for the purposes of review no part of this publication may be reproduced without prior written permission from the publisher.

Motorbooks International is a certified trademark, registered with the United States Patent Office.

The information in this book is true and complete to the best of our knowledge. All recommendations are made without any guarantee on the part of the author or publisher, who also disclaim any liability incurred in connection with the use of this data or specific details.

We recognize that some words, model names and designations, for example, mentioned herein are the property of the trademark holder. We use them for identification purposes only. This is not an official publication.

Motorbooks International books are also available at discounts in bulk quantity for industrial or sales-promotional use. For details write to Special Sales Manager at the publisher's address.

Library of Congress Cataloging-in-Publication Data is available

ISBN 0-7603–0190–5

Printed and bound in Singapore.

Jacket front

Fledgling pilot Bob Green, with Old Rhinebeck's publicity co-ordinator Suzanne Hayes in the rear cockpit, manoeuvres in close to the DH Tiger Moth camera platform. Until recently this machine was fitted with a machine-gun mounted on a Scarff ring around the rear cockpit and it is still fitted with bomb racks under the port wing for its airshow work. Civil Fledglings were used by Curtiss flying schools in the late 20s and early 30s and some inevitably found their way to Hollywood to act as bombers in mostly second-rate movie thrillers

Jacket back

Still flying. This beautifully restored Curtiss CW-16E floatplane complete with paddle strapped to the port float arrives at the Sun 'n Fun splash-in at Lake Parker in Florida. Built originally in 1933 as a land plane this machine was fitted with its floats in 1990 for the first time by owner Willy Rott from Delray Beach, Florida. The aircraft is powered by a Wright J-65 five-cylinder radial.

A view of the roomy cockpit of the Bristol F.2b Fighter, affectionately known as the 'Brisfit', shows it has the normal instrumentation for its era. Note the 'spaghetti'-like pipes and taps on the lower right of the instrument panel, which are part of the complicated fuel pressurisation system; the throttle is on the left-hand side of the cockpit. Bristol Fighters saw active service in World War I from 1917 and were very effective fighting aeroplanes. This particular aircraft was built in 1918 and never saw active service in the Great War, but it was operated by No. 208 Squadron RAF in Turkey in 1923.

This picture was shot in 1987 and it was said at the time that two original S.E.5s hadn't been seen in the air together for sixty years. The nearest aircraft is an S.E.5e flown by Tony Bianchi of Personal Plane Services whose company restored the aircraft to flying condition. The 'e' dates from 1919/20 when over 200 were assembled by the Eberhardt Steel Co. in the USA. This machine appeared in films such as *Hell's Angels* and *The Dawn Patrol*, and as a mailplane in *The Spirit of St Louis*. Charles Lindbergh flew this very machine in 1926, one year before his historic solo transatlantic flight. It is powered by a 180 hp Wright-Martin 'e' model which was based on the Hispano Suiza powerplant used in early S.E.5s. Angus McVitie is piloting the Shuttleworth S.E.5a.

3 1502 00483 0012

CONTENTS

ACKNOWLEDGEMENTS

Apart from my special thanks to all those new aviation friends I have been fortunate enough to make during the shooting of this book, I should also like to thank Alan Dunn and Simon Morris of Dunn's Photographic Laboratory for their consistent high quality processing, and Philip Goldsmith of KJP Ltd for his advice and help with my photographic equipment. My thanks also go to Nikon (UK) Ltd for lending me a Nikon F4S camera body at extremely short notice. Fuji Velvia and Fujichrome 100D transparency films were used exclusively for the shooting of this book, and photographed on Pentax 6cm x 7cm and Nikon F4 cameras.

INTRODUCTION

Wind in the Wires attempts to cover the development of manned aircraft from the days of the early pioneers to the late 1930s, illustrated with photographs of surviving original aircraft and replicas. Working on the premise that if they don't fly then they are not real aeroplanes, most of the photographs were taken at the three greatest flying collections in the world which specialise in the early years of aviation. I do not wish to denigrate any of the non-flying museums throughout the world as they are of course a very important factor in saving, storing and collecting aircraft and artefacts for future generations, but to see, hear and smell these old aeroplanes in their natural environment is to respect even more those early designers, engineers and pilots.

In France the Salis Collection was started by the late Jean Baptiste Salis, just after World War I, and has continued to grow under the direction of the great man's son, Jean; in the USA, the testimony to the legend of the late Cole Palen continues with the incredible flying circus and museum based on Old Rhinebeck's switch-back airfield in New York State; and in England the Shuttleworth Collection, started by the late Richard Shuttleworth in the 1920s, continues to flourish under the guidance of the trustees and the skill of their engineers. The far-sightedness of these three leading flying collections has doubtless inspired individual collectors and restorers to speed up restoration projects around the world. All of us interested in aviation history must have noticed the increased number of vintage aircraft venturing into the skies again – some types which we thought we would never see fly. To all of those enthusiastic restorers and proud owners from around the world who fly their aircraft at airshows, a very great thank you from all of us for the enjoyment that we get from seeing them fly.

Although, as its title suggests, this book is really intended to cover aircraft from 1909 until the end of the 1930s, when bracing and external control wires were incorporated into their designs, I make no excuses for including the Hawker Hurricane and Supermarine Spitfire as both were first flown in the 1930s, and the Hurricane of course owes much to the classic biplane the Hawker Hind.

Aircraft development spanning the thirty years from 1909 to 1939, where speeds went from a stuttering 40 mph to 400 mph, must surely be rated as one of the greatest technological leaps in modern history. With this in mind I would like also to dedicate this book to the early designers, engineers and pilots who have brought us through such a short number of decades to the safe, reliable and fast civil airliners and the incredible military machines that we have today.

In the book reference is made to La Ferte Alais, Old Rhinebeck and Old Warden, as well as Salis, Palen and Shuttleworth. The full addresses and location of these collections are given below, and hopefully readers of this book will visit them, as I have done. I promise you won't be disappointed and you'll help to keep these wonderful old machines flying for a long time to come.

The Salis Collection is based on the plateau of La Ferte Alais near the town of Cerny, some twenty-five miles south of Paris. A Saturday and Sunday airshow is held once a year in June. The address is: Amicale J B Salis, 91590, La Ferte Alais, France.

Old Rhinebeck Aerodrome is about four miles north of the town of Rhinebeck in New York State and is a two-hour drive from Manhattan. Airshows are held every Saturday and Sunday from mid-May through until mid-October. The address is: Cole Palen's Museum In The Sky, Old Rhinebeck Aerodrome, Stone Church Road, Rhinebeck, NY 12572, USA.

Old Warden Aerodrome is about two miles west of Biggleswade and thirty miles north of Junction 23 on the M25. Airshows are held on the first Sunday of every month from May until September, but many other extra flying events (including three Sundowner shows held on Saturday evenings) are held throughout the season, so why not write to them for a calendar of events. Please send a stamped and self-addressed envelope to: The Shuttleworth Collection, The Aerodrome, Old Warden, Biggleswade, Bedfordshire, SG18 9ER, England.

ABOVE
The Bleriot XI monoplane is remembered by most people as the aircraft that first crossed the English Channel in July 1909, piloted by its designer Louis Bleriot. An original example is owned by Cole Palen and it is seen here at its home base – Old Rhinebeck airfield in up-state New York. The aircraft, powered by an Anzani three-cylinder engine producing around 25 hp, is 'hopped' regularly. This is just one of three original Bleriots based at Old Rhinebeck.

RIGHT
Two of old Rhinebeck's helpers pose in front of the Bleriot XI. They have changed into period costume for the afternoon airshow – earlier in the day they were to be seen cleaning thick oil off the fuselage of a Curtiss Jenny.

Probably because the World Aerobatic Championships were being held in nearby Switzerland in the summer of 1990, the Salis team decided to build this flying replica of Adolphe Pegoud's aerobatic Bleriot XI to coincide with the event.

Pegoud was the first person to demonstrate aerobatics and 1913 was a momentous year for him and for aviation. He learnt to fly, went to work for Louis Bleriot as an engineer, instructor and test pilot, was the first pilot deliberately to bale out of an aeroplane to test the 'chute, and he gave the first aerobatic display in the history of flight. Unbelievably he achieved all this in five months. Pegoud was kitted out wisely with a parachute and a full safety harness in his strengthened aircraft for his first inverted flight. Accounts from the time state that after attaining about 3,000 feet he pushed the stick forward and performed a negative (out-side) half loop to get the Bleriot inverted; the aircraft was then seen to fly upside down for a short time before entering a positive half loop to escape to normal straight and level flight.

The Salis replica took just over a year to complete, but, not surprisingly, no one has yet volunteered to fly it inverted!

Louis Bleriot is pictured here with the Shuttleworth Bleriot XI! No, not the great man himself, who died in 1936, but his grandson, also named Louis. This quietly spoken Frenchman is checking over the Shuttleworth machine and comparing it with his own. 'Ah, number 14; mine is number 225,' he says as he looks at the small brass plate and strokes the machine as if it were an old friend. 'There are the ventilation holes,' he exclaims as his hands move over the three-cylinder Anzani engine. 'It is a beautiful machine,' he says with a far-away look in his eyes.

It later transpired that Monsieur Bleriot was at Old Warden to check out the Shuttleworth machine so that his own could be made airworthy for an attempt to cross the English Channel on the eightieth anniversary of his grandfather's achievement. His aircraft was flown for the attempt by Gloria Pullan who nearly made it across, but the Anzani engine lost power when only a couple of miles from the English shore. Needless to say the Bleriot and Gloria got wet, but both were recovered from La Manche safely.

Chris Morris, Shuttleworth's chief engineer, gets to grips with this original machine. Total concentration is needed even to contemplate getting near a Bleriot as the thin wing-warping wires can easily remind you that even old aeroplanes can bite.

RIGHT
RIGHT
The Shuttleworth Collection's Avro
Triplane IV replica pictured flying over the
Bedfordshire cornfields is making its way
back to Old Warden. Triplanes were
usually powered (or, more accurately,
underpowered) by a 35 hp Green (water-
cooled) in-line engine, but this aircraft,
built in the 1960s for the movie *Those
Magnificent Men in their Flying Machines*,
has a more modern 105 hp Cirrus Hermes
II engine dating from 1927. Even with this
modern engine, which gives three times
the power, the cruising speed is only
forty-five knots. The top wings are 32
feet in span and the bottom, 20 feet.

BELOW
'The oldest British aeroplane flying
anywhere in the world' – this is the proud
boast of the Shuttleworth Collection for
their Blackburn monoplane dating from
1912. Powered by its original 50 hp
Gnome rotary, this machine still flies
circuits regularly around Old Warden.
Apart from the use of wing-warping for
lateral control this Blackburn design, with
its covered-in structure, shows all the
basics of a modern aircraft lay-out.

Often the first reaction of someone looking into the cockpit of this Deperdussin is, 'Where are the instruments?' Quite simply there aren't any in the conventional sense. But if you look closer you can see a button mounted on the control wheel; this is the engine cut-out switch. There is a fuel contents gauge on the four-gallon fuel tank, which is held in place by leather straps. The two filler caps atop this beautiful piece of metalwork are the castor oil cap (furthest away) and the petrol filler cap. The wing attachment bolts can be seen on the left-hand side of the fuselage, making life easier for a quick wing change for storage or, more commonly in the early days, for replacing a damaged wing.

Outwardly cool but possibly a little nervous, Shuttleworth pilot Bill Bowker checks the controls of the Deperdussin (underpower) as he prepares for his first ever 'hop' in this single-seat oldie. His wealth of experience flying vintage World War I aircraft, classic tail draggers and crop-spraying types has helped to prepare him for this moment; that is if anything can! Wally Berry, who has worked on all the Shuttleworth machines over the last thirty years, holds down the tail as Bill gives the 35 hp Anzani Y-type engine the gun.

ABOVE
The Salis Collection's Deperdussin Monocoque replica is a flying tribute to the French speed seekers of 1912. The monocoque construction means it has a hollow fuselage shell of moulded plywood to make it strong and streamlined. The Gnome rotary fourteen-cylinder engine was modified from two 50 hp Gnomes and achieved 140 hp. By the end of 1912 these racers were hurtling around the skies at over 108 mph, just nine years after the Wright brothers made their first flight into the unknown. The 1913 version of the monocoque powered by a 160 hp Gnome broke the world speed record six times in seven months, the final time at Reims in September 1913 with a speed of 126.66 mph.

LEFT
This very accurate replica of a Morane Saulnier H was built by the Salis Collection for the seventieth anniversary of the death of French World War I fighter ace Roland Garros. In 1915 Garros was the first successful fighter pilot, but before this in 1913 he made the first crossing of the Mediterranean in a Morane H. He also held the world altitude record of 17,881 feet in 1912 in a Morane H powered by an 80 hp Gnome rotary. The Salis replica took just six months and 3,400 man hours to build and is powered by an 80 hp Le Rhone rotary from the period.

OPPOSITE
George Ellis, who is more usually to be found test-flying executive jets for Raytheon Aircraft Company, shows how exposed the pilot is in an Avro Triplane; above his waist he has no protection at all and is completely exposed in the aircraft's slipstream. Although this aircraft is a replica, its designers decided to keep to the original design of wing-warping rather than substitute ailerons which would have been spotted by enthusiasts watching *Those Magnificent Men in their Flying Machines*, the movie for which it was made. This must be the largest flying example of any wing-warped aeroplane in the world.

Even though this Hanriot dated around 1910 is a replica – or copy if you're Stateside – it is beautifully made in the true monocoque tradition. It looks more like a racing skiff and was in fact a natural technology transfer to use for these early boats of the air. The long wooden arm is the pilot's safety rail and it clips across his thighs similar to a modern-day lap strap. In 1910 Hanriot's fourteen-year-old son Marcel was the youngest pilot in Europe.

With silk scarf flapping in the slipstream Bill King taxies this magnificent French design. This aircraft is based at Old Rhinebeck and is powered by a 50 hp Franklin of 1939 vintage. After the demonstration the public are invited on to the field and encouraged to question the pilot. Bill King tells them that there is a pressure plate mounted to the top surface of the wing indicating airspeed, but that he's always too busy just flying the craft to look sideways to see what speed he's doing.

OPPOSITE
The Shuttleworth Collection's Bristol Boxkite replica is a real crowd puller at airshows in the UK. If you've ever been near Old Warden aerodrome and seen this magnificent aeroplane flying on a sunny summer's evening you'll know what I mean when I say 'you feel as if the clock has been turned back to a much more leisurely era'. The aircraft was built by F G Miles Ltd for the film *Those Magnificent Men in their Flying Machines*, and it featured as the Phoenix Flyer. Boxkites were originally powered by 50-70 hp Gnome rotaries; this example has a 90 hp Lycoming.

So what is the reader's definition of an antique or classic aeroplane? Perhaps parts of the fuselage dating from the past automatically make it an original in some people's eyes; perhaps, and better still, if it was found with its original engine. The odds are, though, that most of the airframe and wings will need new wood, wire and metal fittings, and new fabric, and the engine, if severely corroded, will never run again – so can it be classed as an original?

Well the Shuttleworth Collection's Sopwith Triplane was built completely from scratch for them by the Northern Aeroplane Workshop, as closely as possible to the original drawings that still existed. Not a very good candidate for an 'original' classification you'd think. The twelve-man volunteer workforce started 'cutting wood' in 1973 and finally delivered the machine to the Collection in 1990. Its 130 hp Clerget rotary engine was made from two original engines and fitted a few days later at Old Warden.

The case is therefore clear-cut you'd think – the aircraft is a copy or reproduction with an original engine. Well that's how it would have rested if that

great old man of British aviation Sir Thomas Sopwith hadn't got involved at the project's inception. He was so enthused with the project and the attention to detail achieved that he solved the identity problem once and for all – his pronouncement (close to his hundredth birthday) was that the aircraft was a 'late production model' and that it should be given the production number of 153 some seventy years after No. 152 had rolled off his production line in 1917!

This project was obviously a special case because of Sir Thomas's involvement, but some builders/restorers have started their rebuild with little more than the pilot's seat and a few fittings to base their 'original' on. Thus authentication has become increasingly important as more and more 'restorations' are being rebuilt around the world. When 'old' aeroplanes come up for private sale or auction the value of the machine is determined by its unique history (it might have been flown by a famous pilot or seen 'action' in a famous battle), the numbers of the same model surviving and the current popularity of the type.

LEFT
When the Shuttleworth Collection advertise their Sundowner shows they really mean it. This Avro Triplane replica is being taxied to the hangar at Old Warden well after dusk (in fact at about 9.45 pm on a beautiful summer's evening).

BELOW
Despite the seventeen years of building by the team, flight testing didn't really get into full swing until 1992, held up largely by snags with the Clerget engine. The NAW team led by pensioner Eric Barraclough decided to paint the aircraft as N6290 *Dixie II*, a machine flown by Cdr Arnold of No. 8 Squadron RNAS in 1917. The aircraft is pictured here landing after its third test flight on 16 May 1992 in the hands of John Lewis, the Collection's chief pilot. The aircraft is now flown regularly at Shuttleworth airshows. The NAW team is typical of volunteer aircraft restorers around the world; having spent seventeen years building the Sopwith Triplane they are now well into building a Bristol M1c monoplane for the Collection. This World War I design should appear in the skies over Old Warden in 1996 if all goes well.

Amongst the many famous aircraft types from World War I the Sopwith Camel's record really does match up to the myths and legends surrounding it. Entering service with the first RAF squadron in the summer of July 1917, just sixteen months later thirty-two RAF squadrons were equipped with them. In the intervening months RAF Camels were responsible for a record 1,294 enemy aircraft destroyed, which is the largest total of aircraft shot down by one aircraft type on either side during the Great War. Officially known as the Sopwith F1 when it came into service, the pair of Vickers machine-guns which were faired under a hump were responsible for the aircraft's Camel nickname by its crews. Due to the popularity of the name it was eventually made official. Compared with its predecessors the Camel was an unforgiving machine in the hands of young, low-time pilots, but in the hands of the more experienced it was one of the deadliest 'dogfighting' machines dating from World War I.

This original aircraft is privately-owned and was rebuilt by Tony Ditheridge, boss of AJD Engineering of Suffolk in England; it is currently based at Old Warden. The pilot is Stuart Goldspink, who has more than 5,000 hours of tail dragger experience under his belt; he now spends the majority of his hours flying Boeing 757s and 767s for a living.

The Shuttleworth Collection's Sopwith Pup was originally built in 1920 and was the last of ten civil-registered, two-seater Sopwith Doves off the production line. It was registered as G-EBKY and was bought by Richard Shuttleworth in 1936 and converted into its predecessor, a World War I single-seat Pup. The aircraft's colour scheme was changed for the 1993 season after the machine's 'onion field' adventure.

The Pup, which was officially known as the 'Scout' by the RFC and the 'Type 9901' by the RNAS, acquired its name, so the story goes, when Brigadier-General Sefton Brancker saw the machine for the first time and his reaction was 'Good God! you're 1½ Strutter has had a Pup!' The nickname of course stuck with the pilots and ground crews from both services. To the Pup falls the distinction of being the first aircraft to land at sea. It was flown by Squadron Commander Dunning RNAS onto the 228-foot forward flying deck of HMS *Furious* in August of 1917.

The risk of flying old aeroplanes is always with us, and in August 1991 the Shuttleworth Collection's Sopwith Pup shed its nose and side cowlings while displaying at its home field.

The aircraft was piloted by Bill Bowker who for a split second must have wondered if his propeller had gone as well as the cowlings. Fortunately there are good flat fields to dead-stick into at the end of Old Warden's main runway and Bill managed to clear a low fence with minimal damage to himself and the aircraft by landing in an onion field. The cause of the accident was traced to the cowling retaining cable which had come adrift in flight, and this has since been modified with a new system of brackets and bolts to supplement the cable. The aircraft was flying again at the start of the 1992 season.

For those who say that these old aircraft shouldn't be flown at all because of their historical rarity, they are referred to the original aims of Richard Shuttleworth 'that every item in his collection should be made to work, run or fly in the way it did in the hands of its original designer'

Pieces of cowling still fall from the Pup as the 80 hp Le Rhone rotary engine quits.

BELOW
At rest in the onion field. Closer inspection later confirmed that the cowlings had come off very neatly with minimum damage to the wings and fuselage, and, even more surprisingly, no damage was sustained by the engine.

RIGHT
The cockpit of Cole Palen's Fokker Dr.1 Triplane replica is basic but very practical; the only original part of the aircraft is the tachometer. The red plastic gun is the firing mechanism for the twin Spandau machine-guns; the rat-tat-tat rapid explosions are caused by oxyacetylene gas being ignited.

BELOW
John Barker, chief pilot to Cole Palen's Collection, is also known as the Black Baron to the crowds at Old Rhinebeck. His mount, a Fokker Dr.1 Triplane replica, is one of four owned by the Collection; although one of them was crashed a few years ago it is proudly exhibited in a museum hangar in its pranged state.

Trailing black, sooty smoke the Black Baron has taken a 'hit' during the dogfight routine enacted at Old Rhinebeck every weekend throughout the summer and autumn. A permanently 'crashed' S.E.5a smoulders beneath. The Fokker Triplane is extremely manoeuvrable and the type was the lord of the skies in 1917 when it was made famous by the Red Baron – Baron Manfred von Richthofen, who was also killed in one. No original Fokker Triplanes have survived to the present day but the dozen or so replicas that are still operated around the world confirm the interest in the legend of the Red Baron.

LEFT
The cockpit of the Sopwith 5F.1 Dolphin is still warm and smells of the oil which escaped from its 150 hp, seventy-four-year-old Hispano Suiza engine after taking part in a dogfight over Old Rhinebeck. The stocks of its two Lewis guns can be seen either side of the cockpit, mounted on a horizontal swivel.

BELOW
Complete with white helmet, Cole Palen is seen here flying his Sopwith Dolphin on an air test on 8 September 1990. A fortnight later the aircraft suffered an engine failure in flight and pilot Dick King was lucky to walk away from the wreckage with cuts and bruises.

BELOW
This view of the Sopwith Dolphin shows the fixed twin Vickers machine-guns above the engine cowling and the twin Lewis guns mounted one either side of the pilot. Built originally as a fighter, it entered service with the RFC/RAF in 1918. During this time Dolphins were used most successfully as ground attack aircraft, in particular during the German spring offensive.

OPPOSITE
A close-up of Old Rhinebeck's Sopwith Dolphin during an engine check – note the brown paper parcel attached to the port undercarriage strut; it contains the famous Palen homemade soot dispenser, for smoke effects.

This small Albatros D.Va insignia trademark is positioned at the top of the rudder belonging to Old Rhinebeck's replica and the squadron symbol on the fuselage is shown below.

The agricultural-looking but highly functional cockpit of the Albatros D.Va is dominated by its tachometer, a genuine German model.

Eddie Usinwicz pilots the epitome of German World War I fighting aeroplanes: the Albatros D.Va, near Old Rhinebeck. This replica is powered by a 175 hp Ranger instead of the 160 hp Mercedes fitted to production D.Vas. The Albatros formed the backbone of the German Air Force and von Richthofen scored almost seventy-five per cent of his victories in this type.

LEFT
The tail skid assembly of Old Rhinebeck's
D.Va gives the only clue to its civil identity.

N 12156
PALEN ALBATROS D.Va
SER. N° 17 D 7517

BELOW
Two German classics from World War I: an
Albatros D.Va and a Fokker Dr.1 Triplane
form up in the gathering gloom of a
threatening rainstorm for the camera ship
– Cole Palen's Curtiss Fledgling.

'We'll put you over there sir, if you don't mind,' signals the ground handler to Angus McVitie, the pilot of Shuttleworth's Royal Aircraft Factory S.E.5a. This classic fighter from the Great War is powered by a 200 hp Wolseley Viper V-8 and is armed with a pair of forward-firing, fixed Vickers machine-guns, and a single Lewis gun mounted on top of the wing centre section. F904 is painted in the colours of No. 56 Squadron RAF.

This picture was shot in 1987 and it was said at the time that two original S.E.5s hadn't been seen in the air together for sixty years. The nearest aircraft is an S.E.5e flown by Tony Bianchi of Personal Plane Services whose company restored the aircraft to flying condition. The 'e' dates from 1919/20 when over 200 were assembled by the Eberhardt Steel Co. in the USA. This machine appeared in films such as *Hell's Angels* and *The Dawn Patrol*, and as a mailplane in *The Spirit of St Louis*. Charles Lindbergh flew this very machine in 1926, one year before his historic solo transatlantic flight. It is powered by a 180 hp Wright-Martin 'e' model which was based on the Hispano Suiza powerplant used in early S.E.5s. Angus McVitie is piloting the Shuttleworth S.E.5a.

F904 vents lubricant from the top
starboard wing during checks on its 200
hp Wolseley Viper V-8 engine. The engine
cowling has been taken off for ease of
adjustment during this test run, and from
this angle the S.E.5a's armaments can be
seen clearly. John Stoddart, the
Shuttleworth engineer hanging half out of
the cockpit, is not a happy man though –
after this engine run there were more
questions unanswered than before.

BELOW
Cole Palen took five years to restore the
SPAD XIII which was the first of his six
aircraft to fly, and a lot of people warned
him that he would probably kill himself in
it. With only limited tail dragger time he
taught himself to fly it. Those early flights
were eventful, usually ending up in ground
loops, and on one occasion he and the
aeroplane finished up only a few feet
from a closed hangar door. He flew it
regularly up until 1971. The aircraft was
restored again in 1989 but the engine is
'hollow' because, as an Old Rhinebeck
helper reasoned, 'if we made it totally
airworthy, Cole might want to go fly it
again!'

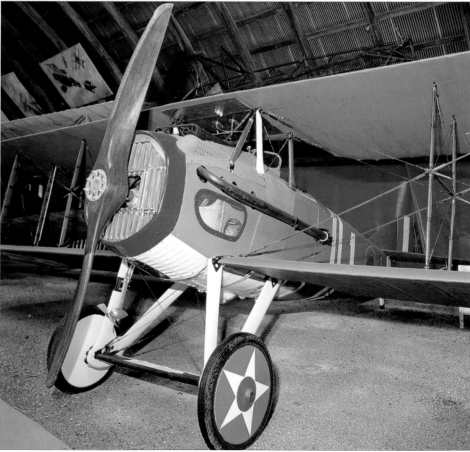

LEFT
LEFT
Old Rhinebeck's original Nieuport X now houses an 80 hp Le Rhone rotary instead of its original 130 hp Clerget. The aircraft was acquired in a swap with the National Air & Space Museum for Palen's Nieuport 28.

BELOW
Getting 'em started is the same problem the world over. Here John Barker, chief pilot and engineer to the Old Rhinebeck Collection, attempts to start the Nieuport X – the guys with rearward facing caps (just right for the period) don't seem at all bothered by the delay. The Nieuport was originally brought to the States by French fighter ace Captain Nungessor in 1924, and it bears French markings and Nungessor's own insignia on the fuselage.

Old Rhinebeck's Curtiss Jenny is a JN-4H model; the 'H' denotes that it is the 150 hp Hispano Suiza-powered version which makes it a rare breed amongst the majority of very few Jenny survivors, most of which are powered by Curtiss OX-5s. In the mid-1920s the US Government proclaimed that the wood-and wire-braced construction of the Jenny was unsafe, so thousands of these machines were scrapped. The name 'Jenny' comes from the corruption of the

designation JN, and as the affectionate name suited this big, lumbering and reliable biplane it stuck.

OPPOSITE
Old Rhinebeck's Curtiss JN-4H Jenny 38278 has been flying since 1969. It didn't arrive in this condition though, for back in 1957 Cole Palen had bought it as 'sight unseen'. It was supposed to be a Standard J-1, but from the nineteen major components of a wrecked machine which arrived in a boxcar from Winter Haven in Florida, it turned out to be this very rare JN-4H minus its 'Hisso' engine, wings and radiator.

Like all old aero engines the Jenny's 150 hp 'Hisso' still throws a lot of oil – so on highdays and holidays it gets the soap and water treatment. The Jenny turned out to be the right aircraft at the right time when the Great War started in 1914. Even fabled and respected specialist writers on Curtiss aircraft agree that the JN-4 evolved by trial and error rather than inspired design. Originally sold to the US Army as an observation aircraft, it was rapidly realised that they were more suited to the role of a trainer. In fact over ninety-five per cent of all US and Canadian pilots met the Jenny at some time in their training during World War I. Over 10,000 Jennys were produced and many of the JN-4Ds, produced from 1914 until just after the Great War, were fitted with the 90 hp Curtiss OX-5 engine. Many were later rebuilt as the 'H' version with the Hispano Suiza 150 hp powerplant.

Dick King lifts off in Cole Palen's JN-4H to start the fun in the air. Reminiscent of the great barnstorming stunts of the early 1920s, the one-and-a-half-hour Sunday show at Old Rhinebeck features many great stunts performed by this Jenny. The one the crowd really loves is when a dummy of Trudy Truelove, the heroine of the show, is whisked off on the end of a rope attached to the Jenny's wings and later unceremoniously dropped onto a

'motorised' haystack. Of course the real Trudy then appears from behind the haystack to tumultuous applause. As

Cole Palen said, 'We encourage the audience to cheer the hero and boo the villain.'

A view of the roomy cockpit of the Bristol F.2b Fighter, affectionately known as the 'Brisfit', shows it has the normal instrumentation for its era. Note the 'spaghetti'-like pipes and taps on the lower part of the instrument panel, which are part of the complicated fuel pressurisation system; the throttle is on the left hand side of the cockpit. Bristol Fighters saw active service in World War I from 1917 and were very effective fighting aeroplanes. This particular aircraft was built in 1918 and never saw active service in the Great War, but it was operated by No. 208 Squadron RAF in Turkey in 1923.

Bristol F.2b D8096 taxies out for take-off minus its gunner. The Lewis gun mounted on a scarf ring in the rear cockpit was operated by the observer back-to-back with the pilot. The pilot had a fixed Vickers gun firing through the arc of the prop. In fact the term 'fighting back-to-back' could very well have originated with this type as the term is a very apt way of describing the teamwork needed between the two-man crew when involved in a dogfight.

Old Rhinebeck's Fokker Dr.1 Triplane replica takes off with the Black Baron (John Barker) on board. The smoking S.E.5a is a stage prop.

This Shuttleworth Collection Brisfit is powered by the world's oldest Rolls-Royce aero-engine – a 275 hp RR Falcon III, V-12. The Bristol F.2b sounds like a well-oiled sewing machine when taxying. The long exhaust pipe running the length of the port side up to the observer's position must have been very useful for a little bit of warmth when coming back from a mission over the trenches in the depths of a European winter; the only other protection from the elements is the thin fabric covering the fuselage.

Triplane in trouble? Well, not really – the smoke is coming from a parcel taped to the port tail strut of this Fokker Triplane replica, part of Old Rhinebeck's World War I flying circus.

Fokker Dr. 1 Triplane and Albatros C II replicas taxi along the flight line at La Ferte Alais. Both were built by the Salis Collection for film work. The all-red Triplane, painted as the aircraft flown by the Red Baron, Manfred von Richthofen, was built in 1977 and is powered by a seven-cylinder 145 hp Warner engine. The Albatros C II is, as they say in France, a 'cocktail': it is made from parts of a DH 82a Tiger Moth and powered by a 130 hp DH Gipsy Major. Two of these were built in 1977 and are still based at La Ferte.

OPPOSITE
Sopwith Pup N5152, civil registered G-APUP, is powered by an 80 hp Le Rhone rotary and was built mainly from original parts by Desmond St Cyrien, of Redhill, England. After the twenty-five-minute air-to-air photo sortie when this picture was taken, and over a steaming mug of tea, the pilot of the Pup, the legendary Neil Williams, seemed more relaxed than usual and had a broad grin on his face. When asked why he was looking so happy he said: 'Well, that's the longest flight that we've managed so far – the previous flight had ended up as a forced landing on a cricket pitch.'

In 1917 Pups belonging to the Royal Naval Air Service were the first aircraft to take-off and land on ships at sea. In service from 1916, Pups carried a single Vickers gun which fired through the arc of the prop, and even though they only had an 80 hp engine up front, they were very light and agile and were effectively flown up to altitudes of 15,000 feet.

From the tail on, the Sopwith Pup's beautifully tapering fuselage can be seen. This Pup, owned by the Shuttleworth Collection, carries the serial of the prototype Pup, number N5180, and is civil registered as G-EBKY. It was the last of ten Pups converted to civil two-seat Sopwith Doves on the Kingston-upon-Thames production line in 1918. It was acquired by Richard Shuttleworth in 1936 and was reconverted to a single-seat Pup at Old Warden.

One of the two beautiful Salis Collection Morane A 1 replicas which made their debut at La Ferte in 1978. Originally powered by 150 hp Gnome Monosoupape 9N rotaries, these 1917 fighting scouts were very fast and manoeuvrable. Over 1,000 of these parasol-winged monoplanes were built, with a maximum level speed of 140.5 mph and excellent visibility from the cockpit. They entered service in 1918, and were as revolutionary as the Sopwith Triplane had been a year earlier. In the 1920s Alfred Fronval, Morane's chief test pilot, looped a total of 1,111 consecutive times in five hours in an A 1.

The only original airworthy Morane Saulnier A 1 currently flying is Cole Palen's example at Old Rhinebeck. He bought two from the Wings and Wheels Museum auction in 1981. This one, MS1591, was restored to flying condition, and as the other was only semi-complete it was decided to rebuild it as a Morane Saulnier N Bullet.

A spinning 160 hp Gnome rotary produces a sharp noise like a chainsaw and has more than enough thrust to pull ground handlers off their feet, which always makes a Morane A 1 a thrilling sight of man trying to tame a machine. As can be seen here, it is so powerful it needs considerable strength and skill when ground handled on Old Rhinebeck's uneven surface. Over 1,200 were built and fifty-one were purchased by the US for use as pursuit trainers.

The flat, longish take-off of this original Morane A 1 has to be seen to be believed. Just to see this one stunning machine in the air was worth the air fare across the Atlantic as far as this writer was concerned. The forward fuselage is of metal construction and the rear of spruce. With its parasol wing and strong inverted strut wing bracing system, the A 1 is not only fast but a very sturdy machine.

The world's only airworthy original World War I German two-seater to survive to the present day is Shuttleworth's Luft-Werkehrs-Gesellschaft CVI or, as it's better known, the LVG CVI; 1,100 were built during 1918 and mainly used as reconnaissance and artillery observation aircraft, but they could also carry a small bomb load of 250 lb. In fact, on one raid over London during the late part of the Great War six bombs were dropped on London from an LVG, injuring six civilians. These large, heavy and not very manoeuvrable biplanes, powered by 230 hp Benz six-cylinder in-line engines, were sitting ducks for RAF S.E.5as. This actual machine was forced down by a pair of S.E.5as of No. 74 Squadron RAF in August 1918, even though the LVG had a single fixed Spandau machine-gun firing forward and a movable Parabellum gun operated by the observer.

OPPOSITE

The LVG's cockpit, polished to a Chippendale-like finish, is roomy and has a neat but sparse instrument layout and all of the basics are there: ASI, altimeter, tachometer, water temperature and oil pressure gauges. But what's it like to fly? A 'very heavy Tiger Moth' was the nicest thing that any of the Shuttleworth pilots were prepared to say.

With its ground hugging twin-boom layout and tractor engine, Old Rhinebeck's Caudron G.3 replica must be one of the most unlikely looking aeroplanes ever to achieve flight. Surprisingly, 1,400 of these reconnaissance aircraft were built; most entered French service from 1914 powered either by a 70 hp Renault or an 80 or 100 hp Anzani. Some were also used by the RFC, powered by an 80 hp Gnome. With this see-through, twin-boom configuration you could be forgiven for expecting the machine to be powered by a pusher rather than a tractor engine.

Truly 'wind in the wires', or should it be 'wind between the fabric'? This close-up of the Caudron G.3's top wing illustrates the corset-like ancestry of the trailing edge.

Cole Palen's replica Avro 504K, armed here with four homemade rockets mounted on the starboard struts, was brought to New York State in 1971, but it was built in the UK in 1966 by Viv Bellamy for a motion picture which was never shot. Powered by an original 110 hp Le Rhone, it wears the yellow and black checkerboard colour scheme of a machine built by Morgan and Co. of Leighton Buzzard, England.

The Avro 504's long in-service history dates from 1913 through to the outbreak of World War II when it was used as a classic two-seat trainer by the RAF. But it also has a history as a successful bomber which is not so well known. In November 1914 four Avro 504s bombed the Zeppelin works at Friedrichshafen. Over 8,000 Avro 504s of various types were built, and the aircraft was arguably the greatest training aeroplane of all time.

This original Avro 504K dates from 1918 and is still very much a flying performer at Old Warden. It carriers its correct RAF number of H5199. The rudder and tail control cables are routed out through the fuselage for ease of maintenance and for easy visual pre-flight checks. It is fitted with a 110 hp Le Rhone rotary. In 1989 this aircraft suffered a power loss on finals and force-landed 400 yards short of the runway in a beetroot field. The aircraft tipped over on its nose and finished up with the lower part of the engine buried up to the centre of the prop. Surprisingly, very little damage was done and the aircraft was flying again in 1990.

This Thomas Morse S-4B, now licking its wounds after coming to minor grief at an Old Rhinebeck airshow, is a very rare machine to have survived into the 1990s. The Thomas Morse Aircraft Corporation was founded in early 1917 by the Thomas brothers and the Morse Chain Company in the US. Nine months from start-up the company received its first order for this advanced flying trainer powered by a 100 hp Gnome Monosoupape rotary. They were equipped with either a 0.30 Marlin machine-gun or a camera gun. The US Signal Corps ordered 100 of these aircraft. After the war many S-4s came into civilian hands and were used for air racing and early movie stunt work which took an even heavier toll on their fast diminishing numbers. But in spite of this 'Tommy' survivors number over a dozen today although most of these are the later version, the S-4C. The Old Rhinebeck craft is believed to be the last example of an S-4B.

1920s

First flown in 1927, the Morane Saulnier MS 138 was used as a two-seat primary trainer by the French Aeronautique Militaire; 178 were built for the service and flown until 1935, and another thirty-three were built for civilian use. From this angle the parasol wing bracing wires can be seen passing over the enormous French civil registration of this Salis-owned aircraft.

The Salis Collection's Polikarpov U 2 biplane is about to receive some fuel from this yellow container via a waiting funnel positioned on top of the fuel tank. This large biplane, which has a wingspan five feet longer than a Stearman's, is powered by a Shetshov five-cylinder radial delivering 148 hp.

BELOW
This Morane 138 original, belonging to the Salis Collection, epitomises the end of an era. The wire-braced parasol wing has metal wing spars, but the majority of the airframe is constructed of wood with a fabric covering. The unusual sight of a king post-supported wing on an aircraft dating from the late 1920s makes this aircraft a classic example of one of the last designs to employ this system. This particular aircraft was bought as a wreck in 1967 and was restored to flying condition by the Salis team, making its first flight in 1978. Over the years many private collectors have attempted to buy this aircraft from the Salis Collection, but all have been unsuccessful. The Collection regards the aircraft as too important to their French aviation heritage. Powered by an 80 hp Le Rhone nine-cylinder rotary, the aircraft has a maximum speed of 87 mph and flies very well.

First built in Russia in 1928 and known as the Polikarpov U 2, these aircraft were redesignated P 2 after Polikarpov's death in 1944. Polikarpov U 2 and P 2 production ran for an amazing twenty-five years in which time 40,000 of them were built. Originally powered by a 100 hp M-11 radial but later changing to the more powerful 145 hp version, the aircraft were used by the military in a number of ways: as a night artillery observation platform; in a night propaganda role with loud speakers fitted; and in the 'nuisance raider' role armed with a maximum of 550 lb of bombs. In their civil role they were used as crop sprayers and air ambulances, and there was a version with a cabin for passengers, but the poor pilot still had to sit out in the cold. Polikarpovs were also involved in the defence of Stalingrad during World War II, their main role being that of a morale booster to the besieged citizens.

The Salis Polikarpov now wears the red star of the old Soviet Union, but it came from Yugoslavia and was civilian registered as YU-CNS.

Dating from 1929, the Curtiss Fledgling is described on its Old Rhinebeck information board as 'perhaps an aeronautical dinosaur'. It certainly is a character aeroplane. This aircraft is a civilianised version of the US Naval N2c-1 trainer. It's big (39½ feet wing span), slow and steady making it an ideal bomber for Old Rhinebeck shows. It is powered by a 220 hp Continental, whereas the original models would have been powered by 220 hp Wright J-5 radials. It is pictured here over the mighty Hudson River, near the Kingston Bridge only a few flying minutes from Old Rhinebeck.

''We're back!' signal the four delighted passengers in the huge front cockpit of this beautifully restored New Standard D-25, dating from 1929. Pilot Eddie Usinwicz has to lean out of the cockpit and look around the enthusiastic passengers to park the aircraft safely. At twenty-five dollars per person for a fifteen-minute joyride over the beautiful Duchess County countryside, this is a trip not to be missed. You are seated two-by-two and share a lap strap with your neighbour. This might not be everybody's idea of fun, for as one relieved first-timer put it, 'I'd rather there was a lid on top of the plane so you can't fall out'; but you can bet he was the first in the queue to buy a 'T'-shirt with the legend 'I survived my ride in the D-25'.

John Barker, chief pilot and engineer to Cole Palen's Collection, taxies in with the last batch of joyriders before the start of the airshow. John has to rush off to change into his Black Baron's outfit and make-up before the 'silliness' starts, as he calls it.

Four more lucky white-helmeted and goggled passengers get airborne as a hazy green blur, which is Old Rhinebeck, whizzes past the New Standard D-25.

Carl Erickson rests by the tail of the Davis D1-W. These aircraft were first conceived as the 'American Moth' by the Vulcan Aircraft Company in the late 1920s. A high performance two-seater (this one is powered by a 125 hp Warner), they came into prominence when ex-auto maker Walter Davis acquired the manufacturing rights. Dating from 1929, the D1-W was popular with sportsmen and stock plane racers of the era. About sixty of these high wing monoplanes were built.

Yes, this is still the Davis D1-W, N532K. Yes, it is a monoplane. I know it now has two sets of wings! But this is Old Rhinebeck! In full view of the public, during the morning of a show day, all the aircraft are bombed up, loaded with rockets, or, as in this case, a false bottom wing. You see a 'lunatic' has to fly it. You don't see? Well during the show a 'lunatic' tries to take off in it and the ground crew grab the wings to try and stop him. Hey presto, the fake wings come off and the aeroplane becomes airborne! Still confused? Aaaw, go 'n' see the show.

The striking Davis aircraft logo as it is applied to Old Rhinebeck's Davis D1-W just aft of the rear cockpit.

OPPOSITE
G-AAHY, a DH 60M Moth, is owned by
Mike Vaisey in England. Here the ground
crew are folding the wings back so that it
can be pushed back into a limited parking
space on the flight line at Old Warden. The
suffix 'M' denotes a 'metal' Moth, thus

known because this model, dating from
1928, was a strengthened version of the
Gipsy Moth. The metal fuselage made the
aircraft heavier by about 62 lb and the
engines available for these machines
ranged from 90 hp A.D.C. Cirrus III's to
120 hp Gipsy IIs.

Test pilot Angus McVitie, more used to
flying aircraft near the 'cutting edge',
gets to fly something a little quieter at Old
Warden: the classic de Havilland DH 60G
Moth, G-ABAG, which was built in 1930.
The prototype DH Moth took to the skies
for the first time on 25 February 1925
powered by its then newly developed and
lightweight 60 hp Cirrus 1 engine.

Shuttleworth's DH 60X Hermes Moth is powered, as its name suggests by a 105 hp Hermes II four-cylinder in-line engine. It has been based at Old Warden since 1932 and was the first aeroplane ever bought by Richard Shuttleworth. This really is a beautiful machine to fly in with the wind in your hair and a nice long exhaust stack to warm your hands on along the starboard side of the fuselage.

From this angle the Sopwith Dove's slight wing sweep is visible. Stuart Goldspink, who has done all of the test and display flying on the machine so far, has logged about three-and-a-half hours and has flown a passenger once, but the performance 'wasn't very exciting', he said.

Roger Reeve's beautifully restored Sopwith Dove is historically a very important machine as it is the direct link between the end of World War I hostilities and the much happier times of the 1920s. This civilian two-seater was developed from the classic single-seat Sopwith Pup fighter dating from 1916. A production batch of ten Sopwith Doves was produced from 1919 through 1920, of which three were sold in Australia and Tasmania.

The fuselage of this aircraft was found in Sydney, Australia, and shipped to England where it was restored by Tim Moore and his team at Skysport Engineering Ltd. in Bedfordshire. The stern posts and trimmer mechanism as well as many other parts were taken from G-EBKY, the last British registered Dove which gained its C of A in 1927. It is powered by an original American-built 80 hp Le Rhone.

Shuttleworth's diminutive de Havilland DH 53 Hummingbird is an aeroplane with a reputation for giving some pilots a permanent limp. The cause of most of the aircraft's sudden descents back to terra firma can be traced to its powerplant, a 1930s vintage, 34 hp A.B.C. Scorpion horizontal twin. This prototype DH 53 was the first light aircraft design from de Havilland and was built to compete in the *Daily Mail* light aeroplane trials of 1923 held at Lympne, Kent. De Havilland's test pilot, Hubert Broad, astounded those present when he looped and rolled this very low powered aeroplane at the 'trials'. Unbelievably eight of these machines were ordered for the RAF and two were especially modified with a hooking mechanism above the pilot's head to enable him to fly off and back to the mother airship, the R-33.

G-EBHX is pictured here in late 1993 after two years of airframe and engine restoration, which was sponsored by Birmingham International Airport plc as their international code, 'BHX', is the same as the last three letters of the Hummingbird's registration. Test pilot Bill Bowker poses the aircraft on the Hummingbird's longest flight so far: a twenty-five minute session. The airspeed read off from the photoplane estimated the Hummingbird's cruise speed at an astounding 90 mph, some 25 mph faster than that recorded by Desmond Penrose when he was test flying the machine in the 1970s.

One of G-EBHX's many memorable moments from the past was the flight from Stag Lane to the Brussels Aero Exhibition in 1923 by Alan Cobham, a distance of 150 miles. He achieved the flight in a time of four hours while consuming only ten shillings (50p or 78 US cents) worth of fuel. However, on its return flight due to a headwind Cobham was overtaken by a Belgian goods train and, as I guess even that great man's pride could only take so much, he landed at Ghent and had the aircraft dismantled and shipped back to England from Ostend.

OPPOSITE
Richard Shuttleworth's first aircraft acquisition was this de Havilland DH 60 Moth bought at Brooklands in 1932; it is pictured in front of his birthplace, Old Warden Park, which is only a couple of minutes' walk from Old Warden's hangars. Richard re-engined the aircraft in 1933 with a 105 hp Hermes II, four-cylinder upright in-line instead of its original 65 hp Cirrus I unit. The machine is registered as a DH 60X Hermes Moth and it is the unchallenged boast of the Collection that G-EBWD has lived at one aerodrome for longer than any flying aeroplane in aviation history.

Three aptly-named English Electric Wrens (after Britain's smallest bird), built in 1921, made their names in the 1923 *Daily Mail* light aeroplane trials at Lympne in Kent. The aim of the designers was to produce a lightweight airframe with very good fuel economy. One of the 'Lympne' aircraft achieved 87.5 miles on a gallon of fuel, but there is no record of a Wren getting any higher than 1,200 feet on its tiny horizontal twin 398 cc A.B.C. engine.

In 1993 the Shuttleworth Collection decided to enhance the Wren's performance by bungee launching the aircraft at two of their air displays. A launch crew of twelve was required: four on each end of the bungee, one member on each wingtip and two lying prone

holding the tail; while the pilot guns the engine, a thirteenth member signals the release for the pullers. The aircraft has reached heights of between eight and ten feet so far on these hops and is fast becoming one of the most popular items at a Shuttleworth show.

The apparent ground-hugging Wren taxies quite quickly back to the starting point for another bungee launch.

1930s

This Comper CLA 7 Swift, dating from 1932, has probably one of the most interesting histories of any early British aircraft. It is pictured here being flown by the late Bill Woodhams who had the mammoth job of disassembling the aircraft in the late 1960s because of glue failure in the wooden joints. He finished up with, as he put it, 'a heap of firewood in the corner of the hangar' from which gradually emerged this beautiful restoration job. Before Bill owned the machine, CTF had been flying around the Indian subcontinent in the 1930s. Owned from new by a tea planter from Assam, Mr Alban Ali, the aircraft was known as the 'Scarlet Angel'. One of the many exploits Mr Ali attempted was to fly from Calcutta to Heston, England. On the way he decided to compete in the Viceroy's Cup Air Race in Delhi and achieved 124 mph over the 699-mile course, finishing second. Mr Ali continued his journey after the race but had to give up when the Scarlet Angel's 75 hp engine sucked in too much sand and gave out at Abu Sueir in Egypt. After this the aircraft never went back to India and continued its journey to England by sea.

Belgium's answer to the DH Tiger Moth was the Société Stampe et Vertongen SV.4B. Jean Stampe, a Belgian World War I pilot, and his partner Maurice Vertongen, an ex-fighter pilot, formed their famous aircraft company in 1923 and became the Belgian agents for the DH 60 Moth in 1927. Their first efforts at building their own two-seater training and touring aircraft bore a great deal of similarity to the DH design. Their SV.4B of 1937 was similar to the DH Tiger Moth if you didn't look to closely, but in fact the Stampe design had many improvements: both upper and lower wings were moved forward and swept back and the fin was enlarged to the configuration that we know today. Thirty Stampe SV.4Bs were produced for the Belgian Government before World War II, but the majority of the 997 eventually produced were made under licence by SNCAN in France after the war. This example is an SV.4C, powered by a 145 hp Gipsy Major. It is based in England, and 350 Stampes are known to exist to this day.

During the Comet restoration a conscious decision was made by Shuttleworth engineers under the guidance of British air-racing veteran Ron Paine to include a modern avionics suite and to fit an electrically-powered undercarriage and a better crew escape system. It was felt that this would minimise some of the risks endured by the original pilots of the aircraft, particularly during take-off and landing. However, the Comet still has its large black and yellow manual undercarriage retraction wheel on the starboard side of the cockpit, in case of emergencies. Test pilot George Ellis says he tried lowering the undercarriage with his hand wheel and it took about a hundred pushes to get the required 'two greens'!

The wonderful sight of Shuttleworth's historic de Havilland DH 88 Comet Racer *Grosvenor House* flying at Old Warden is something that we may have seen for the last time. Because Old Warden's grass runways are too short for the Comet to land safely the aircraft has been operated out of Hatfield ever since its rebuild to flying condition in May 1987. When London Business Aviation closed their facility at Hatfield it would have left the Comet without a hangar, so on 22 May 1994 the aircraft arrived back at Old Warden via the A1, on two forty-foot flat-bed trailers.

The aircraft's wings were re-mated with the fuselage that same day so that the Comet could stand on its own wheels again and the aircraft has been grounded at Old Warden ever since. The aircraft will be kept airworthy though and taxied at some of the Shuttleworth shows until hopefully a new flying base can be found for it.

Old Rhinebeck – Rainbow – Great Lakes 2T-1MS, 1931 biplane.

Roaring away under the power of its 125 hp Menasco Pirate is Cole Palen's Great Lakes 2T-1MS fitted with balloon tyres for rough-field work. Designed as a two-seat sport/trainer in the late 1920s, this very popular and agile aircraft is one of about 200 built before the 'Great Depression' interrupted the original planned production run of over 700. The Great Lakes Company was founded in 1929 and set up dealerships all over the USA and even had overseas branches. Other models of the 2T-1 were powered by either Cirrus or Ensign engines. The name re-emerged in the 1960s as the Great Lakes Aircraft Company selling plans and materials for the scaled-down, self-build version of the sport/trainer known as the Baby Great Lakes. Then for a time in the early 1970s over 100 full-sized sport/trainers were produced, the final variant being the 2T-1A-2 powered by a 180 hp Lycoming. Guess you can't keep a good design down!

These four classic American trainers are owned by Bob Mitchell of Birmingham, England, and operate under the airshow name of 'PT-Flight'. Leading the formation is a Fairchild PT-23 powered by a Continental W.670 radial and built by the Howard Aircraft Corporation, followed by two Ryan PT-22 Recruits with Kinner 160 hp radials up front; in the rear is a Vultee BT-15 Valiant, better known to its crews as the Vultee 'Vibrator'.

Bob Mitchell gets his 160 hp Kinner radial started with a 'swing' from Shuttleworth's Chris Morris. You don't have to have particularly good eyesight to recognise a Kinner-powered machine as the normal rattly noise emanating from the engine is heard long before the aircraft comes into view.

This Ryan PT-22 is painted up to represent an aircraft based at Lindbergh Field, California, in its heyday. It's now based at the slightly less glamorous Coventry Airport, England.

Although American registered, this Ryan PT-22 Recruit, flown by owner Bob Mitchell, has been on the British airshow circuit for the last four or five seasons. Over a thousand Recruits were built for the USAAF, plus twenty-five for the Dutch Navy. Production ended in 1942.

OPPOSITE
The classic planform of the Supermarine Spitfire still brings a nostalgic tear to many an eye wherever it performs. This example belongs to the Battle of Britain Memorial Flight and is flown by RAF-serving pilots. The BBMF also operates the only airworthy Avro Lancaster on this side of the Atlantic, a Douglas C-47 Dakota, five Spitfires and two Hurricanes. The aim of the unit is to remind us Brits of 'our finest hour' and to act as a recruitment tool for the RAF.

With nearly 1,500 hp of Rolls-Royce Merlin roaring away up front, Shuttleworth pilot George Ellis heaves this clip-winged Spitfire Mk Vc off Old Warden's grass runway at about 100 mph. AR501 was built by Westland Aircraft, better known today for their helicopters, and flew with No. 310 (Czech) Squadron at Duxford, Cambridge, in 1942. Wearing the markings of that unit, this Spitfire is the only one still flying with an original three-blade prop.

The low angle of the sun in this shot picks out the wing armaments and shows the clearance of the twin exhaust stacks from the engine cowling. The pilot has his cockpit canopy in the back position while taxying. The Spitfire Vc, of which 2,447 were built, was designed as a fighter bomber, and this model could carry either one 500 lb bomb under the fuselage or two 250 lb bombs under the wings. Its firepower could also be varied as the Mk V was fitted with the 'universal wing' which could take either four 20mm machine-guns, eight 0.303s or two 20mm and four 0.303 guns together.

Spitfire Vc, AR501, flown by Shuttleworth chief pilot John Lewis, comes in close to the cameraship, on this occasion a DHC 1 Chipmunk with the front canopy back for unrestricted photo shooting. The Chipmunk is flying at its cruising speed of about 110 mph and the Spitfire is just idling along, throttled back to match our speed. At the end of the sortie the Spitfire dropped back a mile or so before overtaking us at speed, making us the centre of a beautiful victory roll. It vanished into the summer haze within seconds, but photoship pilot and photographer couldn't stop yelling 'aggle, aggle, achtung! achtung! SPITFIRE! SPITFIRE!' all the way back to the field.

The Focke-Wulf Fw 44 Stieglitz (Goldfinch) is one of the few to survive in flying condition and is pictured here at La Ferte Alais in 1990. This classic trainer, designed by Kurt Tank (of World War II Focke-Wulf 190 fame) and built for the Luftwaffe as a trainer, was famous as an exceptional aerobatic aircraft in pre-war days.

Shuttleworth's BA (British Aircraft Manufacturing Co.) Swallow 2 makes its low and slow approach to Old Warden. This ditch outside the field is a spot favoured by locals when they want to watch the show for free. The Swallow 2's history can be traced back to the 1927 German Klemm L.25 low wing monoplane. The Swallow is fitted with a 90 hp Popjoy Cateract III, a seven-cylinder radial, and when new these engines gave the Swallow a maximum speed of 112 mph and a cruise of 98 mph.

The Stieglitz, first built in 1932 by Focke-Wulf, was the company's second largest aircraft production run and thousands of budding Luftwaffe pilots were trained on these machines. This example is powered by a 165 hp Bramo-Siemens Sh 14A-7 seven-cylinder radial.

Silhouetted against a fast-setting winter sun, the Percival Mew Gull G-AEXF looks much as it must have done when a young English racing pilot named Alex Henshaw took off from Gravesend on the first leg of his record-breaking solo flight to South Africa. This was the era of map, compass and stopwatch and a star sighting if you were lucky. His lonely exploits flying over vast tracts of Africa, at times not knowing if he was over land or ocean at night, are beautifully told in his book *The Flight of the Mew Gull*. He set off on his 6,377-mile attempt on 5 February 1939,

and in five six-hour stages of roughly 1,200 miles apiece he landed at Cape Town in a total elapsed time of thirty-nine hours and twenty-three minutes. As if smashing thirty-nine hours and three minutes off the existing solo record wasn't enough, he then flew back to England the day after (7 February) in thirty-nine hours and thirty-six minutes (total elapsed time) thereby breaking the Cape Town to England record as well. On the round trip of 12,754 miles he succeeded in knocking sixty-six hours and forty-two minutes off the overall record.

He also broke the record for every stage of his flight and this remains unbroken in the solo classification to this day.

Before Alex Henshaw secured the Cape record in his Mew Gull he was already famous as a pre-war air racing pilot and won the 1938 King's Cup Air Race at an average speed of 236.25 mph in this same machine. It is being flown here at Old Warden on its first public display since restoration, and present-day owner Desmond Penrose displays it in a run reminiscent of a racing pylon turn from a bygone era.

Pictured in October 1990 on its first air-to-air sortie after restoration, the Mew Gull, one of only six built and the sole survivor of its kind, makes a splendid sight in the low sunlight of an autumn evening.

Walter Beech's Beech D.17s, affectionately nicknamed the Staggerwing, is one of the most attractive biplanes ever built. It has a revolutionary electrically operated retractable undercarriage and a 450 hp P&W R-985 engine. It was the 'hot shot' aeroplane of the 1930s. The lower wing is positioned forward of the top wing, and in aeronautical parlance this is known as a negative stagger-wing, but as the word negative promotes the wrong image it became known simply as the Staggerwing. This British-based D.17s (registered N18V) is in the colour scheme of a UC-43. The machine is painted up to resemble one impressed into service by the RAF, as DR628, given to Prince Bernhardt of the Netherlands to fly during his wartime exile in England, hence the 'code' PB1. This actual aircraft was the first Beech 17 (39-139) acquired by the US Army and was the personal aircraft of the US air attaché to London.

The all-time classic Beech D.17s offered that extra bit of luxury for its pilot and three passengers – leather seats, motorcar-type wind-down windows and entrance through a door in the side of the fuselage, like an airliner. With a cruise speed of nearly 200 mph, a climb rate of 1,600 feet per minute and a service ceiling of 21,000 feet, it gave an incredible performance for its day. The many that survive are ex-military machines once operated by the USAAF and the US Navy who used them as liaison aircraft during World War II as UC-43 and GB-1/2s respectively.

Westland Lysanders, or 'Lizzies' as they were known in RAF service, are probably best remembered for their clandestine 'special duties' operations into occupied France during World War II. But in fact this was only a small part of their operational use. They were also used for artillery spotting and reconnaissance, supply dropping, air-sea rescue duties, as target tugs and as lightweight bombers. This aircraft, a Lysander Mk IIIA, V9441/G-AZWT, was owned by the Strathallan Aircraft Collection in Scotland when this picture was taken in 1986; it is being flown by Duncan Simpson, an ex-BAe Harrier test pilot.

As well as the Mew Gull, Desmond Penrose also owns this other magnificent machine from the 1930s. His Arrow Active II, G-ABVE, is pictured waiting its turn in the Old Warden programme after the Shuttleworth Collection's Miles Magister (see here in the Active's prop disc) finishes its routine. This Active II has also been restored to a concours finish, picking up prizes wherever it appears. It is the only Arrow Active II ever built and was first flown in 1932 powered by a 120 hp DH Gipsy III engine. The engine and fin had been changed over the years but

Desmond has restored it to its original 1932 configuration and he can still get a spritely cruise speed of 128 mph out of it.

Shuttleworth's Parnall Elf, G-AAIN, dating from 1932, is the sole survivor of the three originally built. Pictured here on finals to Old Warden at sunset, the machine was once owned by Lord Apsley and based at Badminton. It was acquired by the Collection, in non-flying condition, in 1951. Designed by Harold Bolas and built by George Parnall and Co., the Elf was designed as a two-seat tourer. After the other two Elfs were destroyed in flying accidents no more were built.

Emerging from the lower wing of the
Parnall Elf are the rod-operated 'poles'
connecting to the ailerons; they disappear
into the rear of the upper wing. Note the
lack of bracing wires as this machine's
wings are supported by a 'Warren Girder'
construction.

It's almost too dark for photography as the Parnall Elf comes in to land at one of the Shuttleworth evening flying displays. On these occasions flying doesn't start until 6.30 p.m. and goes on until dusk; this is usually the best time to see the very old aircraft displayed as not only is the air far less turbulent, but the low angle of the sun makes for good pictures.

Three Boeing PT-17 Stearmans taxi out for take-off at the Wings over East Texas Airshow at Gregg County airport. These hard-working and versatile aircraft have operated as trainers, crop-dusters and barnstormers as well as aerobatic and joy riding aircraft ever since they were built back in the 1930s, and a lot more of them are still going strong. Most of them are owned by private collectors now. Originally fitted with a 220 hp Continental, they have, in their time, been fitted with all types of monstrous engines such as the 450 hp Pratt & Whitney or even a 300 hp Lycoming.

This de Havilland DH 89A Dragon Rapide, which was owned by Mike Astor at the time, is dressed up as an RAF Domini air ambulance from World War II. It is powered by two 205 hp DH Gipsy Queen III in-line engines. Only about four Dragon Rapides are now airworthy out of the total of 728 built between 1933 and 1946. They were operated in every conceivable role where reliability and ruggedness were acquired. Mike sold the aircraft in 1991 and tragically the new owner was killed and the aircraft completely destroyed in a freak accident soon after.

What better way to fly than in one of Mister Piper's Cubs on a lovely summer day. This machine, painted in Netherlands Air Force camouflage, is in fact a Piper PA-18 Super Cub 135 masquerading as an L-18.

OPPOSITE
Brian Woodford's immaculate Dragon Rapide is painted in the colour scheme of the pre-war King's Flight and is treated royally wherever it performs.

This Hawker Hurricane IIc, PZ865, was the last of 12,780 Hurricanes produced in Britain by 1944. The first Hurricane flew for the first time in November 1935, and it was such a giant leap forward from the biplanes like the Gloster Gauntlets and Gladiators that it replaced that the Air Ministry ordered 1,000 of them within twelve months. Although the Hurricane and Spitfire will always be synonymous with the Battle of Britain, it is interesting to note that more enemy aircraft were shot down by Hurricanes than all of the other wartime defences put together during this battle. This machine is now the only Hurricane operated by the Battle of Britain Memorial Flight as their other Hurricane was badly damaged in an accident in 1991.

The BBMF's other Hurricane IIc, LF363, is pictured near the Imperial War Museum at Duxford. This aircraft has led the Battle of Britain Remembrance Day flypasts over London since 1945. Hurricanes, powered by their Rolls-Royce Merlins, were used in all theatres of World War II: at the defence of Malta, in the Western Desert, in Burma, and, modified with tail hooks as the Sea Hurricane (one of which is being rebuilt by the Shuttleworth Collection), operating off aircraft carriers. When they were operated in a ground attack role the IIc's were armed with four 20mm guns and could carry up to 500 lb of bombs.

Waiting for 'the off' is the only flyable Hawker Hind in the world. Owned by the Shuttleworth Collection, it is seen here armed with four dummy 125 lb bombs. This machine is now painted in No. 15 Squadron RAF markings, but it didn't look like this when it was brought over land some 6,000 miles from Afghanistan in the 1970s. The machine is one of a batch of eight Hinds delivered to the Royal Afghan Air Force in 1938, some of which flew until 1956.

Shuttleworth engineer Andy Preslent pushes the Hucks Starter's drive bar into the Hawker Hind's propeller dog prior to start-up. The Hucks is based on a Ford Model Two-Ton chassis. Driver Chris Morris doesn't need any distractions when he's performing this type of start-up, for although as soon as the engine fires the Hucks drive bar is automatically pushed back about a foot, the driver must then select reverse gear on the old Hucks to avoid a very embarrassing splintering noise.

As the Hind taxies out to the holding point, the crackle of its 640 hp Rolls-Royce Kestrel engine grabs everyone's attention. As you look at this picture, half close your eyes, imagine an enclosed canopy for the pilot and take off the top wings; what have you got? The basic Hawker Hurricane shape.

The Fairy Swordfish, known affectionately to everyone who flew in or serviced it as the 'Stringbag', was virtually obsolete when war broke out in 1939. This example, a Swordfish II, LS326, is one of two flying examples in the UK proudly operated by the Royal Navy Historic Flight at RNAS Yeovilton. These carrier-borne aircraft were slow, stable, and very manoeuvrable, and therefore ideal platforms for launching torpedoes and bombs. They were involved in many famous naval engagements during World War II, in particular the night attack on the Taranto dockyards when two Italian battleships were sunk and another severely damaged as well as a cruiser, two destroyers, some seaplane hangars and oil storage tanks. Another famous engagement took place in the Atlantic where the Royal Navy were hunting the German battleship *Bismarck*. Swordfish, from HMS *Ark Royal* and *Victorious*, attacked the huge vessel and disabled its steering gear with their air-launched torpedoes – the *Bismarck* was then finished off by the fleet.

Who else but the Royal Navy would take the salute while standing to attention in the back of an airborne Fairey Swordfish? It's always a wonderful sight, and a great crowd pleaser too, when the old 'Stringbag' flies past low and slow with its tail hook down. LS326 currently wears this Norwegian Campaign colour scheme to great effect.

Shuttleworth's Hucks Starter wouldn't win any automobile beauty contests but it is a very efficient way of starting up pre-war aeroplane engines. The vehicle is driven here by the late Wally Berry, who worked as an engineer with the Collection for thirty years. He was well used to starting the Hawker Hind, Avro Tutor, Bristol F.2b and Avro 504K with this labour-saving contraption. Dating from the 1920s, the Hucks was over hauled by de Havilland apprentices in the 1950s and donated to the Collection.

Bill King taxies his DH 82a Tiger Moth at Old Rhinebeck. The aircraft carries the false British registration of G-ACDA – the real CDA is being rebuilt by Richard Biddle so Bill is toying with the idea of repainting his as G-ACDB. Bill King is a very active pilot on the Old Rhinebeck scene and is currently restoring Cole Palen's Puss Moth in his garage at home. In his spare time he has also rebuilt a Luscombe 8A Silvaire as well as this Tiger.

The crew of this de Havilland DH 82a Tiger Moth prepare to start up. The machine is painted up as a RCAF trainer from World War II. The forward door is down and the folded 'blind-flying' hood is attached to the 'students' rear cockpit.

OPPOSITE
The Shuttleworth Collection's Tiger Moth is dressed up as a RAF trainer dating from the late 1930s, but in fact the first Tiger Moth flew in 1931. It was developed from the DH 60 Moth and originally had a 120 hp Gipsy III inverted in-line engine. The structure was toughened-up for RAF use and the wings were staggered for ease of exit by parachute; the engine was also changed to a 130 hp Gipsy Major. Over the years over 7,000 were built in Canada, Australia, New Zealand and of course at Stag Lane and Hatfield in England.

Helmet, goggles, a vintage Tiger and limitless visibility make open cockpit flying a real joy – in this case Oliver Wells, one of the Shuttleworth trustees, is having fun.

Bill King, silk scarf flapping in the slipstream, takes off in his own Tiger Moth. The machine's colour scheme represents an aircraft operated by the de Havilland School of Flying.

Tiger Moths in war-paint are very popular in the UK, but this one, T7909/G-ANON, carries the correct military serial it wore when in service with the RAF. The passenger in the front seat is enjoying himself taking shots through the struts and wires.

G-ABLS is probably the finest example of a Puss Moth to be found anywhere in the world today. The long undercarriage fairings can be turned in flight to act as airbrakes. These machines were usually powered by a 130 hp Gipsy Major I giving the machine a comfortable cruise of 100 mph. Many of them flew on record-breaking attempts during this era; one of their most famous pilots, 'Bert' Hinkler, was finally killed in one when crossing the Alps in 1933 en route to Australia, after he had previously made many record-breaking flights. Another pioneer of the time, Jim Mollison, had a 160-gallon long-range tank fitted in the cabin giving him an unrefuelled range of 3,600 miles.

Angus McVitie smiles broadly as he brings the DH Puss Moth in to another 'three pointer' landing at Old Warden. The DH 80A, to give it its correct title, first flew in 1930, and as some of de Havilland's customers were looking for a two-seater enclosed cockpit machine, the Puss Moth was born. This machine is on a 'long loan' to the Shuttleworth Collection and saw RAF service during World War II as ES921. Some 259 Puss Moths were built between 1930 and 1933, but the aircraft suffered several major accidents early in its career – it was found that wing failure could occur in turbulent conditions.

Bill Bowker, complete with flat cap, looks the part as he demonstrates the aeroplane that the smart executive was flying in the mid-thirties. A total of 165 of these DH 87B Hornet Moths was built from 1934 onwards as a modernised version of the DH 60 Moth two-seater. The large thirty-five-gallon fuel tank was positioned behind the pilot's seat, and on a shelf above it was space for two large suitcases. Even with all of this on board as well as two people, the Hornet Moth had a claimed useful range of 600 miles.

As 1990 was the fiftieth anniversary of the Battle of Britain, the Shuttleworth Collection decided to repaint their unique airworthy Gloster Gladiator in camouflage for that year's flying season. The only squadron of Gladiators operated in the Battle of Britain belonged to No. 247 Squadron RAF based at Roborough. They were responsible for the defence of the naval dockyards at Plymouth during the hot summer of 1940 because Spitfire and Hurricane squadrons were not up to strength. The Shuttleworth machine, N2308, pictured here is flown by George Ellis during the hot summer of 1990.

The last of the British fighting biplanes, the Gloster Gladiator, although virtually obsolete at the outbreak of World War II, gave a pretty good account of itself in the early war years. Gladiators were operated from a frozen lake in Norway in 1940, and three, named *Faith*, *Hope* and *Charity*, helped in the defence of Malta; they were operational in the Western Desert campaign and also in Greece. Shuttleworth's machine was built in 1938 and is powered by a Bristol Mercury 840 hp nine-cylinder radial. It has a maximum speed of 253 mph and an initial climb rate of 2,300 feet per minute and is armed with four Browning machine-guns; as pilots who have flown it will tell you, 'it's very impressive and its manoeuvrability will take your breath away'.

Monsieur Henri Mignet designed in the early 1930s the Pou-de-Ciel (Sky Louse), or 'Flying Flea' as it is known in the UK, as a homebuild aircraft with the objective of making them easy to build and safe and easy to fly by their home constructor/ novice pilots. Unfortunately, not all of the builders used materials suitable for aircraft construction and some of the machine's inherant control problems managed to damage pilots and their machines. In the UK close to 100 Fleas had been registered by 1937, but, with wind-tunnel research at RAE Farnborough and in France showing that the design needed refining, 'Pou' mania subsided on both sides of the Channel until after the war. Many variants of the basic Pou-de-Ciel have been built and flown successfully since then. At a recent fly-in at Marennes in France organised by the great man's son Pierre Mignet, over forty Pou variants turned up at the event, but not all of them by air.

OPPOSITE
Still flying. This beautifully restored Curtiss CW-16E floatplane complete with paddle strapped to the port float arrives at the Sun 'n' Fun splash-in at Lake Parker in Florida. Built originally in 1933 as a land plane this machine was fitted with its floats in 1990 for the first time by owner Willy Rott from Delray Beach, Florida. The aircraft is powered by a Wright J-65 five-cylinder radial.

The one and only Granger Archaeopteryx was built and designed by the Granger brothers from Nottingham, England, making its first flight in 1930. The two brothers were lace manufacturers by profession and wanted to learn to fly in their own machine as so many other home builders have done over the decades ever since. After seeing the Westland-Hill Pterodactyl perform in 1926 the brothers, with the professional help of C. H. Latimer-Needham, embarked on their own semi-tailless design. The aircraft is powered, or to be accurate underpowered, by a 32 hp flat twin Bristol Cherub engine. Although the aircraft is only taxied these days, back in the 1970s John Lewis, who is now chief pilot at the Shuttleworth Collection, regularly flew the aircraft. As the cockpit is so cramped the throttle is mounted externally on the aircraft. This of course means that the pilot has to fly the aircraft with his elbows out in the slipstream, and as John found when he tried to climb the aircraft out of ground effect still below 200 feet, the machine would not climb until he managed to tuck his elbows in. Even then it took ten minutes to reach 600 feet.

OPPOSITE
As the years roll by the classic Piper J-3 Cub two-seater seems to get more and more popular; on a hot day what better way to stay cool than by removing the horizontal split window/door and feeling that warm Florida breeze in your face as you splash down on to a remote lake? This cub is fitted with EDO 1140 floats making the machine technically a J-3C-65S.

When William T. Piper, an oilman by profession, bought into the Taylor Brothers Aircraft Corporation for $400 in the late 1920s he knew nothing about aircraft except that they were too expensive. Later, when the Corporation went belly-up, Piper bought the assets for just $761 retaining its English-born, self-taught aeronautical engineer, C G Taylor, as president and chief engineer. The Taylor E-2 Cub was first certificated in June of 1931 selling for $1,325, but it didn't sell in the hoped-for numbers. It wasn't until Piper finally bought Taylor out in 1935 and gave Walter Jamouneau his chance to improve the basic design of the aircraft into the J-2 (J for Jamouneau)

that the sales really lifted off, a year later. The Bradford, Pennsylvania, plant produced over 500 J-2s in this first year thanks to the 'hungry' sales team and a fly-away sales tag of $1,270.

The Piper J-3 Cub was 'born' at Lock Haven in 1937 after the Bradford factory had burnt to the ground a few months earlier. Like Henry Ford before him, Piper produced the Cub in only one colour, 'Cub Yellow', complete with black lightning flash along the fuselage. Total production of the J-3 Cub variants is estimated to be just over 20,000 aircraft. Over 2,000 saw

active service in Europe during World War II and over a thousand supported the D-Day landings. Probably the strangest version of the Cub was the bulbous-nosed glider version known as the TG-8, of which over 250 were built. But the best known variants of the Military Cub were the O-59s and L-4s of the Army and the NE-1s of the Navy; over 5,000 of these artillery spotter and scout aircraft were ordered.

The pilots who went to war in a Piper Cub flying at low level and with only the thickness of the doped canvas between

them and an enemy bullet must be true candidates for the unsung hero award of all World War II flyers. These Military Cubs were shipped to war packed in large wooden crates which carried a manifest on the outside of each box. The notice read: 'Aircraft L-4, cost to US Govt., $800; Crate, 1942 M-2, cost to US Govt., $1,200.' In a single year (1946) Piper Aircraft built 6,320 J-3 Cubs, a record for the greatest number of civilian aircraft of a single type produced in any one year, and one which will probably never be beaten.

Building your own homebuilt is difficult enough, but to restore a large 1930s classic aeroplane to flying condition is a mammoth task for a couple of individuals. John Barker (left) built this workshop in up-state New York with the help of his wife Pamela (an ex-DC-8 flight engineer and now First Officer on Boeing 737s) and while living in it built their house next door. As if that wasn't enough they started to restore their Travelair Speedwing D.4D which they bought as a wrecked crop-duster in Oregon. Mix all of that wi th the adventure of the aircraft's overland recovery to New York State, hundreds of hours of research at the Smithsonian into the limited remaining structural plans of the Speedwing, and the search for an

engine to replace the 300 hp Jacobs and you've got a rough idea of the dedication and determination required before you even start restoring an aeroplane. John and Pam's Speedwing was originally rolled out by Travelair on Valentine's Day in 1930 as a D4000 and was one of the last of 1,400 aircraft built by them; the Barkers' machine carries the construction number 1367. The Travelair Company was originally formed by three of American aviation's legends, Walter Beech, Clyde Cessna and Lloyd Stearman, but by the mid-twenties Cessna and Stearman had gone their separate ways leaving Walter Beech in control; as John Barker says, 'this must make my Speedwing the granddaddy of all Beech aeroplanes'.

Restoration took two years to get to this stage. It is now fitted with a Wright R760 J-67 235 hp radial from from an Island Airways Ford Tri-Motor, completely overhauled by Mike Connors in Florida, and should give the Speedwing a cruise of 130 mph. More importantly, though, without its crop-spraying hopper and booms and with the shorter 'speedwings' fitted the machine's climb rate should be phenomenal, and it will need to be to get to its working altitude of 10,000 feet for John's proposed sky-writing activities.

The Miles M.3A Falcon dates from 1936 and is a classic example of a British between-the-wars tourer. With the pilot (in this case Stuart Wareing) sitting on his own up front and space for two passengers sitting side-by-side behind, this surely was the epitome of those 'Bentleys' of the air. Powered by a 130 hp de Havilland Gipsy Major, Falcons cruised at around 145 mph and had a range of 650 miles. The aircraft is now owned by

Tim Moore of Skysport Engineering, one of the leading aircraft restoration companies in the UK, but from new in 1936 it went directly to the Swedish Air Force and did not return to UK ownership until 1962.

Many of F G Miles' designs competed in the air races of the time; the prototype of the Falcon series known as the M.3 was no exception, and in the hands of H L Brook it competed in the 1934

MacRobertson Race from Mildenhall to Melbourne. He and his passengers had a hard time and it took them nearly twenty-seven days to reach Darwin, but on the return trip, flying solo (some five months since leaving Mildenhall) and with extra fuel tanks to give a range of 2,000 miles, he succeeded in breaking the Darwin-UK record in a time of seven days, nineteen hours and fifteen minutes.

The Shuttleworth Collection's version of
the term 'push-back' requires a bit more
muscle power than when the term is used
in the airline industry. The Collection's
chief pilot, John Lewis, hands resting on
the Spit's cannon, helps the ground
engineers to get the aircraft into wind
ready for take-off.

<small>OPPOSITE</small>
Spitfire at sunset! Chris Morris,
Shuttleworth's chief engineer, secures
the mighty Merlin's engine cowlings
before their Mk Vc concludes the sunset
show with a roaring finale. During the long
summer evenings three special Saturday
shows are held by popular demand
starting at 6.30 pm and often going on
beyond sunset.

To give even more authenticity to the Old
Rhinebeck airshows, many vintage
vehicles earn their keep by participating in
the 'ground war'; in this case a couple of
large bombs are attached to this wagon
from the era.

Trudy Truelove, 'our heroine', thumbs her nose as she is kidnapped by the Black Baron and his cronies in a vintage car during the 'madness' on the ground as World War I fighters scrap it out in the skies above them.

This close-up shows the twin Spandau machine-guns that 'arm' the very agile Fokker Dr.1 Triplane replica.

Pierre Loop de Loop's (alias the late Cole Palen) 'ladyfriend', Madame Fifi, runs the lingerie shop on Old Rhinebeck's back lot. She and her chauffeur wait by their Saxon sports car for their cue before re-entering the mayhem that is Old Rhinebeck's Sunday show.

During weekdays and before the crowds arrive at the weekends, Old Rhinebeck aerodrome reverts back to its wonderfully tranquil self. It's more like a farmyard than an airfield, with its own ducks and geese seen here taking a walk away from their pond which has snapper turtles under the surface.

Old Rhinebeck's vintage fire engine is kept very busy during the aerial bombardment routine. One of the homemade bombs, which are dropped from the air, landed on the windscreen of this vehicle a week before this shot was taken. I was asked if I would like to travel out on to the field in this machine during the bombing to take some battle shots. Yes, I said, but only if I could borrow a bombproof umbrella to shelter under!

The late Cole Palen stands in the cockpit of the Sopwith Dolphin replica looking very smart in white overalls and helmet and wearing a backpack parachute. He has just got back from a test flight in the machine.